A GIFT FOR

G000038461

Tun & Dad
Christmas
2003

Helen Exley Giftbooks
for the most thoughtful gifts of all

EDITED BY HELEN EXLEY
ILLUSTRATED BY JULIETTE CLARKE

Published simultaneously in 2000 by Exley Publications in Great Britain,
and Exley Publications LLC in the USA.

2 4 6 8 10 12 11 9 7 5 3 1

ISBN 1-86187-186-4

A copy of the CIP data is available from the British Library. All rights reserved.
No part of this publication may be reproduced in any form. Printed in China.

Exley Publications Ltd, 16 Chalk Hill, Watford, Herts WD1 4BN, UK.
Exley Publications LLC, 232 Madison Avenue, Suite 1409, NY 10016, USA.

Acknowledgements: The publishers are grateful for permission to reproduce
copyright material. Whilst every reasonable effort has been made to trace copyright
holders, the publishers would be pleased to hear from any not here acknowledged.
Pam Brown, Pamela Dugdale & Charlotte Gray: Used by permission. *Sally Emerson:* from
'Back to Work' from Occasional Poets published by Viking Penguin, 1986. Used by
permission of Curtis Brown Ltd. *Lyndene Ginsburg:* from 'A Portrait of American
Mothers and Daughters' published by NewSage Press Inc. *Michele Guinness:* from
'Tapestry of Voices' published by SPCK, 1993. © 1993 Michele Guinness. Used with
permission of SPCK. *'Letters to our Daughters'* © 1997 Kristine Van Raden and Molly
Davis, published by Beyond Words Publishing Inc. *Stuart and Linda Macfarlane:* Used by
permission. *Alexandra Stoddard:* from 'Mothers' ©1996. Alexandra Stoddard. Used by
permission of HarperCollins Publishers and Brandt & Brandt Literary Agents Inc.

A LITTLE BOOK FOR MY
Daughter

A HELEN EXLEY GIFTBOOK

 EXLEY
NEW YORK • WATFORD, UK

WITH PIGTAILS
AND PONY TAILS

"Thank heavens for little girls."
... With pigtails and pony tails,
in jeans and party dresses,
climbing trees, reading books,
sucking gobstoppers and
turning cartwheels, making
friends and breaking friends,
they bring their special charm

into the world, a delight in detail, a tenderness in relationship, a sensitivity to joy and sorrow and spiritual truth....

TENDERNESS
I NEVER KNEW

*[My daughter], from the
moment she was born,
drew from me reserves
of tenderness, protectiveness
and fight I never knew
I possessed. I wanted to
change the world overnight,*

*to make it a safer, easier,
better place for this
miniature woman, this
receptacle of all my dreams
and aspirations....*

MICHELE GUINNESS,
FROM "TAPESTRY OF VOICES"

WHAT IS A DAUGHTER?

A daughter is a new beginning.
A daughter is your excuse
  for making a dolls' house.
A daughter is an awful
  reminder of the way you
  behaved at fourteen.
A daughter is the person
  to whom all that dusty stuff

in the attic belongs.
A daughter is the person
you thought you would stop
worrying about when she hit
twenty-one. But who is still
worrying you silly at forty-five.

PAM BROWN, B.1928

BABY GIRL POWER!

The whisper
of a baby girl
can be heard further
than the roar
of a lion.

ARAB PROVERB

*Wrapped round
her little finger?!
Not at all!!
I <u>wanted</u> to buy her
all those teddies,
dolls, books....*

STUART MACFARLANE

LITTLE GIRL
SHE CAN MUSS UP YOUR
HOME, YOUR HAIR, AND YOUR
DIGNITY — SPEND YOUR

MONEY, YOUR TIME,
AND YOUR PATIENCE —
AND JUST WHEN
YOUR TEMPER IS READY
TO CRACK, HER SUNSHINE
PEEKS THROUGH
AND YOU'VE LOST AGAIN.

ALAN BECK

I AM A FOOL FOR HER LOVE.

NICHOLAS LAZARD

The father of a daughter
is nothing but a high-class
hostage. A father turns
a stony face to his sons,
berates them, shakes his

antlers, paws the ground,
snorts, runs them off into
the underbrush, but when
his daughter puts her arm over
his shoulder and says, "Daddy,
I need to ask you something,"
he is a pat of butter in a hot
frying pan.

GARRISON KEILLOR

LOVE NEVER ENDING

My first thought of you
is of overwhelming,
overflowing love.
An unconditional love,
born out of your being my
firstborn, my vulnerable,
disabled daughter.

WENDY, TO HER DAUGHTER JAIME,
WHO HAS A RARE DISEASE.

I loved you the very first second that I saw your face. But how could I begin to suspect the astonishments held in the bundle of blanket? You are my delight – my never-ending source of amazement!

PAMELA DUGDALE

A MEANING TO LIFE

... a man's life will stay
like a desert — empty
except for sand —
until God endows him
with a daughter.
And I also say that he who
does not have a daughter

*should adopt one, because
the secret and meaning
of time are hidden
in the hearts of young girls.*

KAHLIL GIBRAN (1883-1931)

SHE SMILES

*... my darling girl
Sleeps and smiles and
laughs, her face so
full of curiosity and
magic that I know
the world was
made in her honour.*

SALLY EMERSON,
FROM "BACK TO
WORK"

A Child of Happiness
always seems like an old soul
living in a new body,
and her face is very serious
until she smiles,
and then the sun lights up
the world....

ANNE CAMERON, FROM "DAUGHTERS
OF COPPER WOMAN"

You stormed
into our lives like a tornado.
You toddled
over all our plans.

*You screamed through
our best-loved movies.
You threw up on everything.
You made our lives wonderful.*

STUART AND LINDA MACFARLANE

When the nurse brought my baby in,
I looked into her face and saw myself
— her eyes, her skin, her expressions,
her spirit.... From that moment on my
heart was all hers. I was terrified,
elated, proud, and complete...
all at once.... On that day... we began
our wonderful duet, a blend of heart,
mind, and soul that continues
to this day.

NAOMI JUDD

ADORATION

... Our daughter,
meanwhile, was fast asleep,
one little hand showing
above the bedclothes.
Clenched in it was my heart.

HUGO WILLIAMS, B.1942

*Sometimes, as you lay
peacefully sleeping
in your crib, I would gently
take your tiny hand
in mine just to share
your peace and serenity.*

LINDA MACFARLANE

Daughters are more precious than gold.
More precious than one's dreams, however glorious.
For they are your gift to the world.
They are its hope.
And yours to love.

PAM BROWN, B.1928

"THE HONOR OF BEING YOUR MOTHER."

You've given me more love and joy than most mothers and daughters ever share. I'd do it all again just for the honor and the wonder of being your mother.

LYNDENE GINSBURG
TO HER DAUGHTER STEPHANIE, FROM
"A PORTRAIT OF AMERICAN MOTHERS
& DAUGHTERS"

*I never quite get over the fact
that I have daughters of my own.
Daughters that call up at one in
the morning to tell me they'll be
late home, daughters that get me
out of the bath to tell me they've
passed an exam, daughters that
have me hurtling breathlessly in
from the garden to say "Happy
Mother's Day".*

PAM BROWN, B.1928

FLORAL LEGGINGS AND AN OUTSIZE SWEATSHIRT

The first time I took your advice about what to wear, I thought, "Why am I doing this? I'm going to look an absolute fright in skinny floral leggings and an outsize sweatshirt, the shade of African violets...."

When I saw how pleased you were that I'd trusted your opinion, though, I was glad I'd taken the risk. And when people began complimenting me on my appearance, I charged around like a high-scoring footballer, yelling, "Yes! YES!"

CHRISTINE HARRIS

I WISH YOU WHAT I HAVE
WISHED YOU SINCE YOUR LIFE
BEGAN. MAY YOU NEVER CEASE
TO SEARCH AND CHALLENGE.
MAY YOU DISCOVER WHAT YOU
WANT TO DO — AND DO IT
WELL. MAY YOU ALWAYS FIND
SOMETHING TO DELIGHT YOU.

PAM BROWN, B.1928

MY LITTLE PAL

I was happy that she was all mine, the little person who could absorb all the love pent up inside me. The first time I really knew she loved me back, Melissa was nine months old. During her nap time she somehow climbed out of her crib and crawled all the

way to my room to see me. I said,
"Oh, look. I have a visitor," and
my heart melted, and I got down
on the floor with her.

She was my pal.

JOAN RIVERS, B.1933

LESSONS IN LIFE

You taught me the value of what is really important in life. It wasn't my preconceived ideas of an orderly, successful, "happy" family, perfect as I could make it. But instead I learned the value of investing in lives, something that matters for eternity. I invested in you.

WENDY, TO HER DAUGHTER JAIME,
WHO HAS A RARE DISEASE

Thank you for an excuse to make home-made jam and bake birthday cakes... for bringing back fun to all our lives.

PAM BROWN, B.1928

I REMEMBER

I wonder if you remember
how we loved long days
in the country? How you
laughed when we swung
you in the air?
How we all put on our
bright gloves and went

crunching into the snow?
Your little red bobble hat?
Your tiny boots?
I remember.
I always will.

HELEN THOMSON,
B.1943

NAUGHTY
TIGGERS!

*Rather suspiciously
the words "I didn't…"
were often uttered
before the question
was ever asked.*

GIOVANNI ANDRETTI

Violet Elizabeth dried her tears.
She saw that they were useless
and she did not believe
in wasting her effects.
"All right," she said calmly,
"I'll thcream then, I'll thcream,
an' thcream, an'thcream
till I'm thick."

RICHMAL CROMPTON
(1890-1969)

LITTLE HORRORS

There's nothing wrong with
teenagers that reasoning with
them won't aggravate.

AUTHOR UNKNOWN

If the phone's not engaged
the bathroom is.

AMANDA BELL

When you were twelve
we agreed that as you were
all grown up you should tidy
your own room. That was
seven years ago and you've
still not got around to it.

STUART AND LINDA MACFARLANE

Daughters are inclined to shear off the beautiful hair that you have cherished.
To dye the stubble magenta.

To opt for wearing rags or
worse. To attach themselves to
strange groups and causes.
And stranger boyfriends.
To veer between ecstasy and
misery. To drop bombshells.
They are trying lives on for size.
The daughter you know and
love is still there.

PAM BROWN, B.1928

OOPS!
THE MONEY'S GONE
OOPS!

A tiny, new, baby daughter
is a giant phone bill waiting
to happen.

OOPS!

They say, "a daughter is worth
her weight in gold," they don't

tell you that she will cost you
that amount every month.

OOPS!

Wasn't it strange that when
she started to choose her own
clothes the shopping bill
doubled.

STUART AND LINDA
MACFARLANE

NEVER EVER DULL

Daughters are given to making announcements. I'm joining an ashram. I've signed on to crew a boat to Singapore. I've invited my headteacher to dinner... Today. I'm getting a tattoo. I'm leaving home.

I'm going to be a nun. I'm in love with an Arab sheik. I'm moving back home. I'm having my hair dyed pink. I'm going to settle down just as soon as I've sailed around the Horn....

PAM BROWN, B.1928

FROM GENERATION
TO GENERATION

What must she [my mother]
have thought, after having tried
to "raise me right," when at
seventeen, I stood before her,
teetering on high heels, lips red,
bangs self-cut, with the radio

blasting "Honey Love" by Clyde McPhatter? Probably the same thing I felt when my daughter stood before me with three earrings in each ear, a fuchsia muscle shirt on... bright blue eyeliner, fuchsia lips and nails, and the stereo blasting "Like A Virgin" by Madonna.

ANNETTE JONES WHITE, FROM "DOUBLE STITCH"

*Daughters
do wonderful things.
Not the wonderful things
you expected them to do.
Different things.
Astonishing things.
Better than you ever
dreamed.*

MARION C. GARRETTY,
B.1917

THIS IS THE BEST YOU

I keep an album of photographs of
you as if I could hold on to all the
different yous – the baby, the
toddler, the school girl, the
teenager. But they don't really
matter. Not that much. Because you
are all of them and every time I see
you I think "This is the best time."

PAM BROWN, B.1928

LOVE

WHEN I LOOK INTO YOUR EYES I FEEL MINE SHINE WITH LOVE.

LINDA MACFARLANE

*I wish
that (if ever she sees this)
I could give her [my eldest
daughter, Marianne] the
slightest idea of the love
and the hope that is bound
up in her. The love which
passes every earthly love....*

ELIZABETH GASKELL 1810-1865,
FROM "MY DIARY"

TOGETHER

Within minutes, we're peddling away, the two of us, a genetic sewing machine that runs on limitless love. It's my belief that between mothers and daughters there is a kind of blood-hyphen that is, finally, indissoluble.

CAROL SHIELDS, FROM "SWANN"

WE HAD IT ALL...

... when they put your first child into your arms, perhaps you will think of me — that it was a high moment in my life too when for the first time I held you, a little red bundle, in my arms. And then think of our beautiful three weeks at the seashore — of sunrise, and when we walked barefoot along the beach from Bansin... and when we read books together. We had so many beautiful things together, my child, and you must experience all of them over again, and much more besides....

ROSE SCHLOSINGER (1907-1943), TO HER DAUGHTER ON THE DAY SHE WAS EXECUTED

STRONG AND KIND

*I think daughters
have all been here before —
they change from little children
to wise old women almost
overnight when their families
are confronted by hard times.*

PAMELA DUGDALE

She tried in every way to understand me, and she succeeded. It was this deep, loving understanding as long as she lived that more than anything else helped and sustained me on my way to success.

MAE WEST (1892-1980)

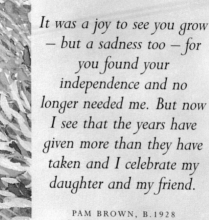

It was a joy to see you grow — but a sadness too — for you found your independence and no longer needed me. But now I see that the years have given more than they have taken and I celebrate my daughter and my friend.

PAM BROWN, B.1928

For all the time, very quietly,
they are changing. Before long, you
are waving goodbye to them at the
school gates. A moment more and you
have a teenager on your hands.
A flicker of time and they are leaving
home — an independent woman.
But holding within them always the

little children that they once were.
Not just the memories of happiness
and fears.... But all those times
beyond recall, when the world was very
new and there was everything to learn.
We have to let go their hands. But the
joys we knew before are part of us all
forever.

PAMELA DUGDALE

THAT PHONE AGAIN

I am watching the television
or sitting down to supper or
just about to get into the bath.
The phone rings. Muttering
terrible imprecations, I pad
along the passage and pick it
up, rehearsing what I am going

to say to the double glazing
sales lady....
But it's OK.
It's you.
Forget the television and
the supper and the bath.
"Hello, love."

CHARLOTTE GRAY,
B.1937

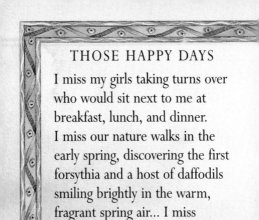

THOSE HAPPY DAYS

I miss my girls taking turns over who would sit next to me at breakfast, lunch, and dinner. I miss our nature walks in the early spring, discovering the first forsythia and a host of daffodils smiling brightly in the warm, fragrant spring air... I miss

hanging out in the library at the children's tables, sitting on brightly painted little chairs. I miss the beach days, the swim meets, the ribbons.

ALEXANDRA STODDARD

LEAVING HOME

DEAR DAUGHTER.
TAKE MY LOVE WITH YOU
NOW AND INTO THE TIME
THAT I WILL NEVER KNOW.
IT IS AS MUCH A PART
OF YOU AS BREATH....

CHARLOTTE GRAY, B.1937

WHERE DID IT ALL GO?

One moment in diapers
the next in jeans,

From crawling to driving
in an instant.
Time disappeared so quickly.
I am blessed to have shared it
with you.

STUART MACFARLANE

Walk gently my daughter
Through life's joys, songs and
triumphs.
For my love will be there in
your heart.
Walk gently my daughter
Through life's sorrows, pains
and woes.
For my love will be there in
your heart.

Walk gently my daughter
Through all life's great
mysteries.
For my love will be there
in your heart.

LINDA MACFARLANE

We have written to each other of our plans, problems, hopes, achievements, disappointments and successes, as well as our day to day happenings. Our letters have been a strong life-line stretched half way around the world: to me they are a continuous message of love and dependence....

IVY SPENDER, MILTON HOSPITAL,
JANUARY 1983

MY HOPES FOR YOU

I wish you so much.
But most of all I wish you
to be your own true self.
To take all the gifts that you
were born with and make of
them marvels of beauty and
ingenuity and astonishment.

CHARLOTTE GRAY, B.1937

*I hope you find joy
in the great things of life —
but also in the little things.
A flower, a song,
a butterfly on your hand.*

ELLEN LEVINE

*I stand by the window and see you
dig in the soil in pants that are worn
at the knees and the bottom.*

    *You have thoughts and adventures
I shall never share. I stand and look
at you and am closer to you than
anything else I know about.*

    *You are part of me which is
completely free.*

LIV ULLMANN, FROM "CHANGING"

... YOU CAN GO
WITHOUT REGRET
AWAY FROM THIS
FAMILIAR LAND,
LEAVING YOUR KISS
UPON MY HAIR
AND ALL THE FUTURE
IN YOUR HANDS.

MARGARET MEAD (1901-1978),
FOR HER DAUGHTER CATHY,
FROM "BLACKBERRY WINTER"